My Aunt A to Z

Fill In The Blank Gift Book

Printed in USA

Published by K. Francklin

Cover Image: Produced by K. Francklin

© Copyright 2015

ISBN-13: 978-1518634031

ISBN-10: 1518634036

I Like Having You As My Aunt Because...

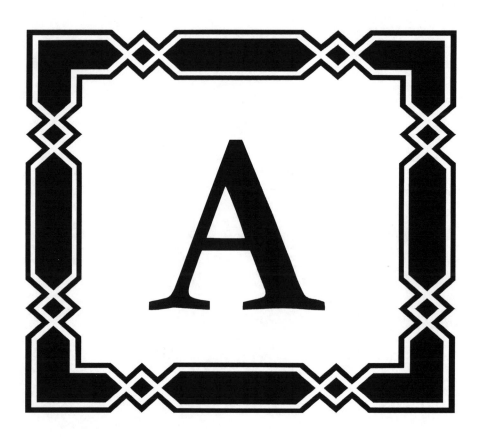

My Aunt is...

A_____

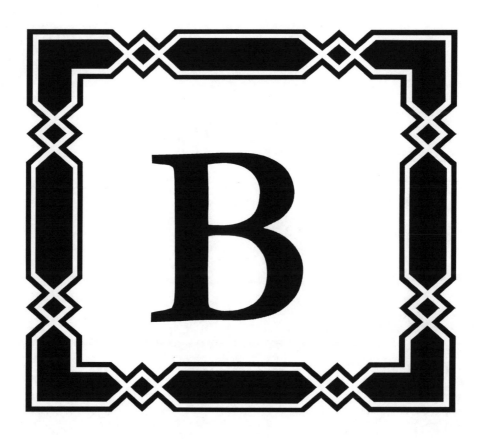

My Aunt is…

B_____

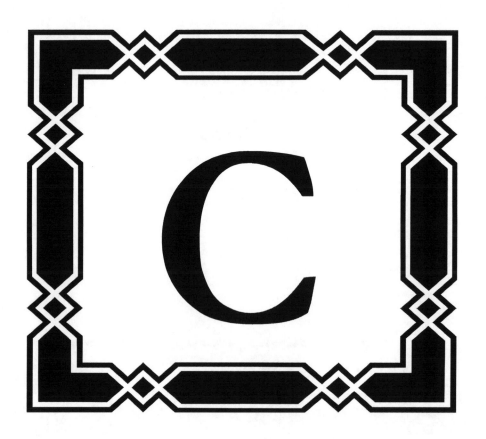

My Aunt is…

C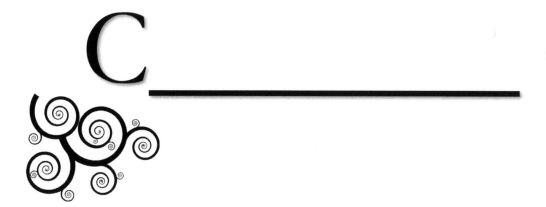

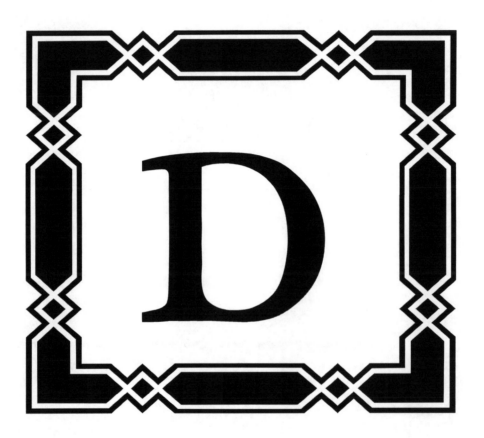

My Aunt is…

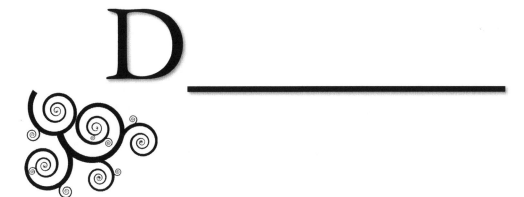

D_____

My Aunt is…

E_____

My Aunt is...

F_____

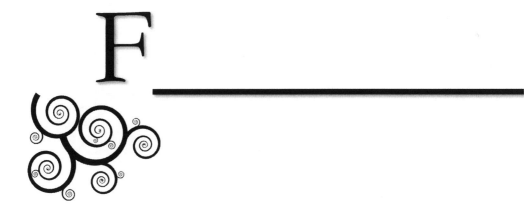

My Aunt is...

G_____

My Aunt is...

H_____

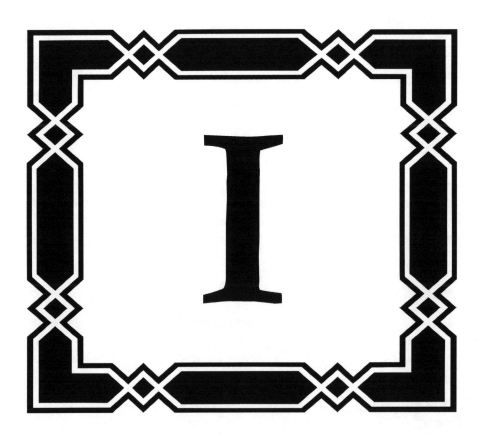

My Aunt is...

I_____

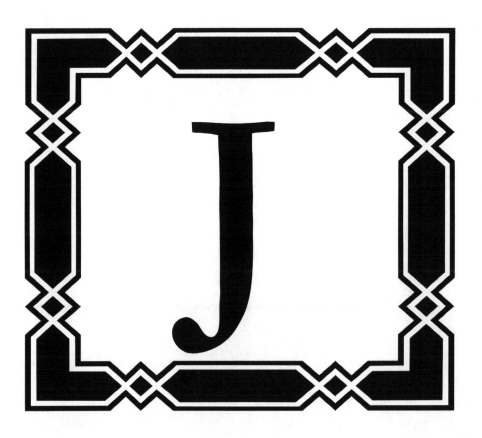

My Aunt is...

J_____

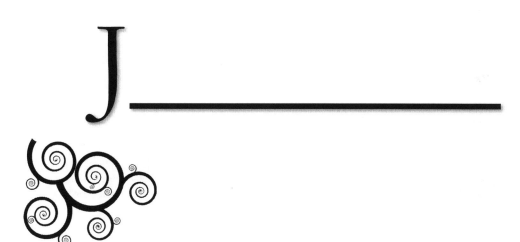

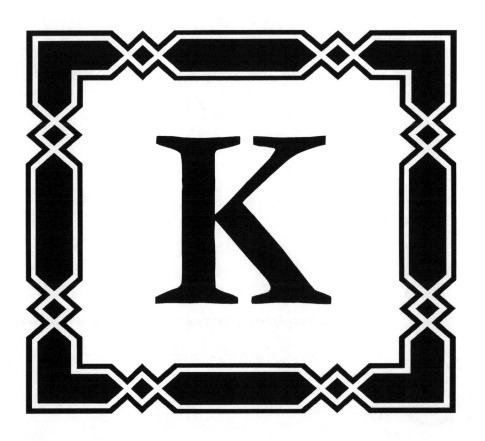

My Aunt is...

K_____

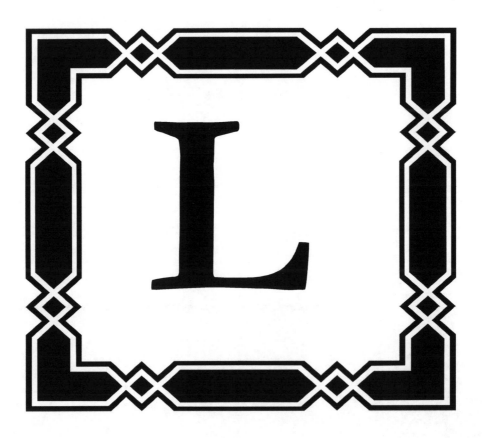

My Aunt is...

L_____

My Aunt is...

M_____

My Aunt is...

N_____

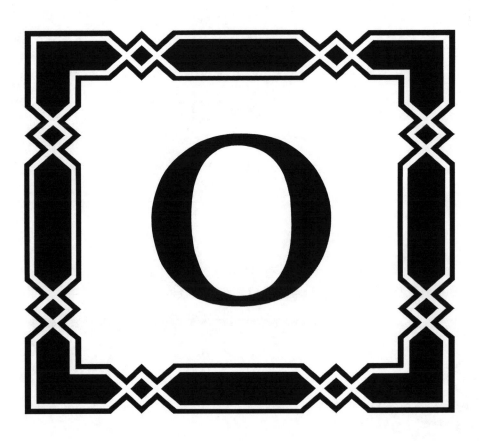

My Aunt is...

O

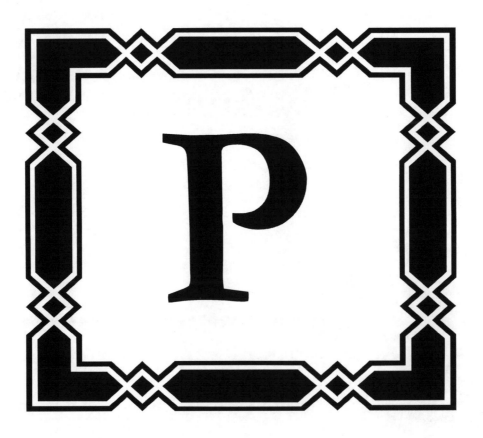

My Aunt is…

P_____

My Aunt is…

Q_____

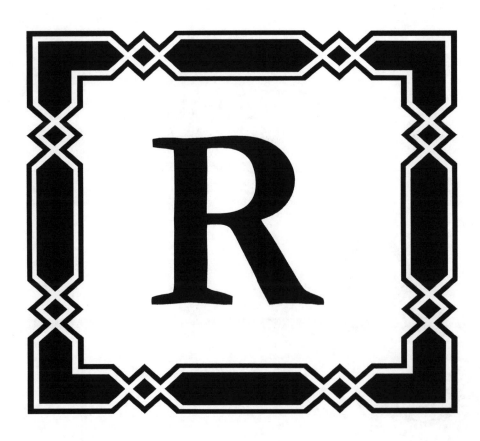

My Aunt is...

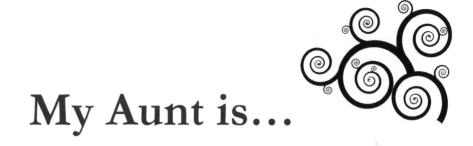

R_____

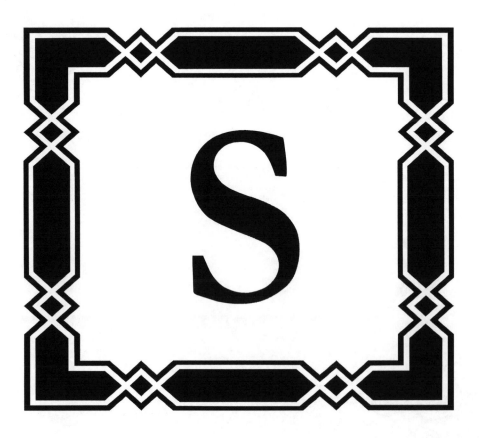

My Aunt is...

S _____

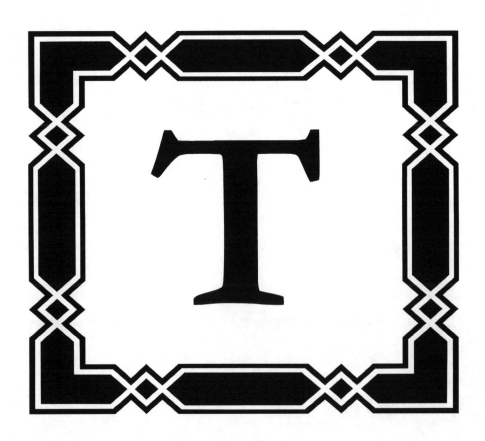

My Aunt is...

T_____

My Aunt is...

U_____

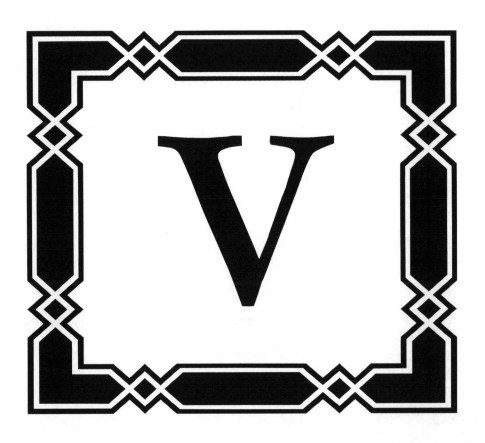

My Aunt is...

V_____

My Aunt is...

W_____

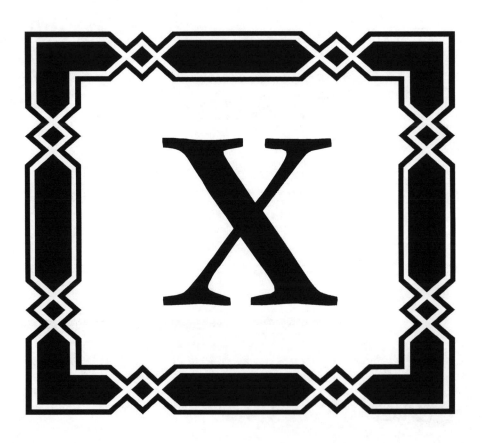

My Aunt is...

X_____

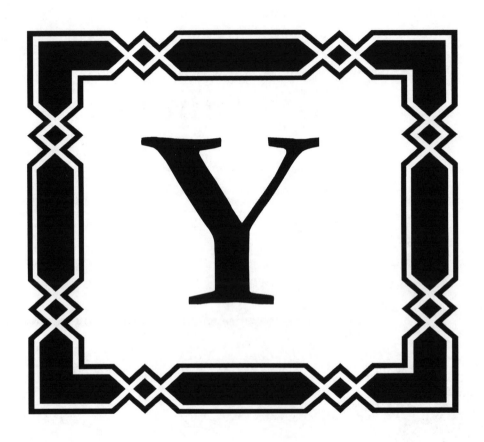

My Aunt is…

Y_____

My Aunt is...

Z_____

Also In This Series

My Dad/Papa A to Z

My Mom/Mum/Mama A to Z

My Son A to Z

My Daughter A to Z

My Husband A to Z

My Wife A to Z

My Sister A to Z

My Brother A to Z

My Uncle A to Z

My Aunt/Auntie/Aunty A to Z

My Grandpa/Grandad/Gramps A to Z

My Grandma/Granny/Nanny/Gran/Nana/Nan A to Z

My Best Friend/Bestie A to Z

My Girlfriend A to Z

My Boyfriend A to Z

My Partner A to Z

Made in the USA
Middletown, DE
07 March 2016